Finding and Marketing to Translation Agencies

A Practical Guide for Freelance Translators

By the author of

How to Succeed as a Freelance Translator

Finding and Marketing to Translation Agencies

A Practical Guide for Freelance Translators

Corinne McKay

ISBN-13: 978-1978136649 (print)

Also available in e-book

Contents

Introduction

Most freelance translators earn at least some of their income from working with translation agencies; many earn the majority, or even all of their income from agencies. This book is intended for:

- Beginning translators who want to dive into the agency market in a well thought-out way; and

- Experienced translators who want to cultivate good relationships with high-quality agencies

If you're going to work with agencies, you must be realistic about the pluses and minuses of the agency market. You can't enter the agency market and expect agencies to be something that they are not. Otherwise, you and your clients may both end up disappointed; definitely a sub-optimal situation.

On the plus side, agencies:

- Can provide you with a steady stream of work. If an agency enjoys working with you, they may keep you busy with an ongoing flow of projects.

- Can free you up to spend the bulk of your time translating, rather than doing non-translation tasks.

- Can decrease your administrative overhead (marketing, client relations, and billing, to name a few). Agencies generally require less non-billable time than direct clients do.

- Are straightforward to find and apply to. If you want to work with direct clients, half the struggle is figuring out what kinds of clients might need you, how to find them, who to contact within the company, etc. With agencies, you don't have that struggle; you can use sources like translators' association directories, Payment Practices (paymentpractices.net), translation portals like ProZ (proz.com) or TranslatorsCafe (translatorscafe.com), or simple web searches ("translation companies in Switzerland," etc.). Once you find agencies you'd like to work for, you simply fill out their application or follow the instructions for sending them your resume.

- May send you work from multiple end clients, thus saving you lots of marketing work.

- Provide somewhat of a safety net. If you get sick or have a major computer problem, or if a translation is suddenly taking three times as long as you expected, an agency client can often get another translator to pitch in...something a direct client may not be able to do.

- Should have your work edited or provide other quality control steps.

On the other hand, agencies:

- Often pay less than direct clients do, sometimes for very similar work. Over the 15 years I've been freelancing, I've seen a shift in the agency market; it's much more difficult to make a decent living at the low end, and there's a lot more competition at the high end.

- May get more involved in your work processes than direct clients do, probably because they know more about translation than most direct clients do.

- Generally need translators in broad specializations like legal, financial, medical, IT, patents, etc. So if you want to translate primarily in an area like art history, human rights, horses, or romance novels (all actual specializations from translators I've met!), you may be out of luck in the agency market.

- May have barriers to entry that seem somewhat arbitrary. Direct clients are generally focused on the result of your work: can you do what they need you to do? Well-qualified beginner translators (i.e. someone with strong language skills who worked in financial services for 20 years, and is now looking for financial translation work) may be frustrated by requirements such as "must have five years' experience as a translator, certi-fication, or a Master's in Translation." Agencies put up those barriers for a reason, but they can create a bit of a chicken-and-egg situation, where you feel that agencies won't hire you without experience, but you don't know how to get experience if no one will hire you.

- May be impersonal to work with. Especially with large agencies, you should expect little to no personal relationship. With some of the largest agencies now assigning their projects exclusively through "come and get it" e-mails or even internal job boards (like their own proprietary Upwork), it's becoming more and more possible to work with large agencies without ever interacting with a human.

- May make you feel like a cog in the machine. I frequently hear this complaint from experienced translators who want a more personal, more trusting relationship with their agency clients; they feel as if they are interchangeable with any other translator in their language pair or specialization, and are frustrated that some agencies don't seem to want, or even be open to, a more personal interaction.

Chapter 1: Before you begin marketing to agencies

If you're planning on working with translation agencies, there are a few factors to consider before you begin. These include:

- **Your language pair(s) and specializations, and how in-demand they are**; with the caveat that there is a potential market for nearly every language and specialization. For example in English to Spanish translation in the U.S. , there is a lot of work, but also a lot of price-based competition. Specializations like financial and sci-tech are going to garner a lot more attention from agencies than a generalist translator will. Small-diffusion languages tend to have fewer projects, but also fewer translators to choose from.

- **Your location**: are there any agencies near where you live?

- **Your level of experience**: are you starting from ground zero, or do you have several years or decades of experience?

- **Your desire for a personal relationship (or not!) with your clients**: smaller agencies generally have a more personal relationship with their end clients, and thus a more personal relationship with their translators.

- **Whether or not you use translation memory tools**: some agencies may require that you use a TM tool, or a specific TM tool, or a specific version of a specific TM tool. This is becoming increasingly true of other pieces of software—QA tools, machine translation plugins—as well.

It's also important to have the right mindset when you're starting an agency marketing campaign. First, marketing to agencies is a bit of a numbers game. When I launched my freelance business in 2002, I applied to over 400 translation companies during my first year in business, and it still took over 18 months before I was earning a full-time income. Second, you have to either accept the agency business model or avoid it. Agencies will take a significant cut of the fee that they charge to the end client. In exchange, they will find the client in the first place, send you the work, and hopefully handle all of the non-translation aspects of the project, such as editing, proofreading, formatting, file prep, etc. If this business model irritates you, you're better off looking for direct clients.

When you work with agencies, you also have to accept that you will rarely (if ever) have direct contact with the end client. In some cases you will have little control over the final version of your translation that is sent to the end client. The agency may have the translation edited without allowing you to review, or even see, the edits. Again, this is a fairly standard agency practice that you have to either live with or avoid.

Chapter 2: Your translation-targeted resume

You'll probably apply to translation agencies in one of two ways:

1. By filling out forms on their website

2. By e-mailing them your resume or submitting it on their website

Having a solid, translation-targeted resume is one of the foundations of your agency marketing campaign. Let's look at some keys to a good resume.

- **Length**: one page is best; two pages are an absolute maximum.

- **Critical information**: include your name, language pairs and specializations in your resume heading. Choose *one name* to use professionally. Do not alternate between your legal name and your nickname, or between one last name and a hyphenated last name.

- **Contact information**: include some type of geographic information (not necessarily your address, but your city or nearest metro area), your e-mail, phone, and website if you have one. Definitely consider purchasing your own domain name, even if you use it only for e-mail purposes. It looks more professional than a free webmail address, and then you never have to change your e-mail address again.

- **File name**: thanks to my friend and colleague Eve Lindemuth Bodeux for this tip. It seems basic, but do not title your resume "Resume.pdf." Include your name, and perhaps your languages ("Corinne_McKay_FR-EN") for example.

- **Objective**: you don't need one. The objective of the resume is clearly to find work.

- **Clients' names**: include them *only* with the client's written permission, unless you worked as an in-house employee, or your name is already on a published translation. Otherwise, just describe the type of client ("A major US-based software company," "A leading Brazilian oil company").

- **Related experience**: only include experience that is truly related to your translation or interpreting work. It's OK to have gaps in your work history. Just omit any unrelated work experience.

See the next page for an example of a translation-targeted resume.

Always put your language pairs in the heading.

Jane Translator

Choose one version of your name to use professionally.

Freelance German to English translator

Specializing in medical and pharmaceutical translations

If you have clear specializations, list them.

Chicago, Illinois

Phone:

You don't need to include your full address, include your city or nearest metro area.

Email:

Website:

I recommend purchasing your own domain name [i.e. janetranslator.com] even if you only use it for e-mail purposes.

Profile: German to English translator specializing in medical and pharmaceutical translations. Certificate in Translation; Member of the Midwest Association of Professional Translators; three years experience as a freelance translator.

Include a clear positioning statement with your language pairs and specializations. Include any translation-specific credentials or certifications.

Recent translation projects:

- Informed consent forms for a major US pharmaceutical company
- Medical records for patients seeking medical care at a major US medical center
- Clinical trial protocols for clinical research organizations

Give some examples, but don't use specifics. Never use client's names without written permission.

Related experience:

2014–present: Freelance German to English translator working with clients in the US and Germany. Specializing in medical and pharmaceutical documents, with ongoing professional development focusing on medical terminology and clinical research protocols.

Education:

Certification in German to English translation, Middle Earth University, 2014

B.S. in Biology, Central Earth University, 2012

Professional affiliations:

Member of the Midwest Translation Association

Computer skills and equipment:

Proficient user of XYZ translation memory tool

Recent professional development:

Online course: Introduction to international clinical trial protocols (University of California, Berkeley, via Coursera)

A few comments on the sample resume on the previous page:

- If you are a beginner, do not lie about your lack of experience, but don't feel compelled to call attention to it either. Don't say "beginner," for example. The client will see your work history and judge for themselves whether you're a good fit for them.

- Even two or three sample translation projects make a positive impression. List these, to give the client an idea of what you translate.

- If you have zero translation experience, you should probably not be looking for paying clients yet. Take some classes, see if you can do an internship at a translation company or with an experienced translator, or translate for pro bono clients to make sure you are confident in the quality of your work before you enter the market.

- If you have zero experience and need some inspiration, take a look at my blog post on three ways to find your first translation clients.

- Under "related experience," list any job that relates to translation, your non-native languages, writing, or your specializations. Don't feel compelled to list the actual years of your employment history or your educational credentials if you don't want clients to know how old you are. You can just say "10 years' experience" instead.

- Listing your professional affiliations and association memberships can help demonstrate your seriousness as a professional translator. List any translation, language, or specialization-related associations you belong to.

- If you own and are proficient in using specialized software such as translation memory tools, desktop publishing software, subtitling or transcription software, etc., list it. Do not list tools that you know how to use but don't own.

- Never list actual clients' names without written permission, unless you worked for the client as an employee or your name is on a published translation associated with them.

- List any credentials related to your specializations: MBA, CPA, licensed attorney, chartered financial analyst, certified medical transcriptionist, registered nurse, etc.

Chapter 3: Finding quality agencies

There are various ways to find quality translation agencies to apply to. In this chapter, we'll discuss:

- Referrals from other translators

- Association directories

- Translation agency rating services

- Simple Google searches

3.1 Referrals from other translators

One of the best ways to find quality agencies to apply to is to ask other translators about agencies that they work with and like. There's a catch: you're best off asking translators who work in other language pairs, because you don't want it to look as if you're trying to poach a colleague's clients. If you ask someone in another language pair, that's not much of a concern. Additionally, if a trusted colleague has worked for an agency for years, you probably don't need to worry about the agency's financial solvency.

Unless you know the other translator well, never make it sound as if you want to use their name as an "in" with the agency (unless they offer). For example, you might say something like, "I'm actively looking for new agency clients. Are there any agencies you particularly like working with, or that you've heard good things about? Of course I would not use your name, I'm just looking for suggestions of agencies to apply to."

With other translators you know well, you might ask whether they would be willing to refer you to any of their agency clients. "I'm actively looking for new agency clients. Would you be willing to refer me to any agencies that you particularly like working with?" Again, make sure you make this request only of translators who you know well, because it's a big leap of faith on their part to allow you to use their name.

3.2 Association directories

Association directories are probably the best way to find large numbers of translation agencies. For example, when I launched my freelance translation business in 2002, I used the paper version of the American Translators Association directory and started with "A," working my way through the alphabet until I had applied to over 400 agencies. You can apply this strategy using the online directory today, or the directory of your country, state, or local translators' association. Two caveats here:

- NEVER use the information in an association directory to directly contact the person (often the CEO) who is listed as the primary contact. Many association directories' terms of use prohibit this, and there's a risk that the information is outdated. Instead, go directly to the agency's website and use the application information you find there. The best place to look for this is a link like "work with us," "freelancers," "join our team," "employment," etc.

- Remember that some translators' associations accept nearly anyone who is interested in the translation industry as a member. So, you must vet the agencies' financial solvency before you apply to them. More on this in the next section!

The great thing about association directories is that you can quickly find hundreds of agencies to apply to. At a minimum, you could use the association directories in your source and target language country/ies as a starting point, and most of these directories are available to the public, not just to the association's members.

3.3 Translation agency rating services

Translation agency rating services such as Payment Practices and the ProZ Blue Board are another excellent way to find agencies to apply to. An advantage of rating services is that they are usually worldwide. Whereas the majority of a translators' association's members are going to be in the country where the association is located, using a rating service allows you to find agencies anywhere.

Let's look at an example of how to use Payment Practices to find highly-rated agencies in Germany (this is not an affiliate deal, I just think that Payment Practices is a great service). After logging in and clicking "Search," you would set your search criteria. Payment Practices uses two rating factors: PPR (payment practices reliability), and TA (translator approval), on a scale of 1-5. In this example, we'll set our desired PPR and TA scores to 4.0 or higher, and our country to Germany.

Search Options

Agency:		All Words (less matches) ⌄
PPR Score:	>= ⌄ 4.0 ⌄	
TA Score:	>= ⌄ 4.0 ⌄	
Country:	hold CTRL to select more than one	
	France	
	French Overseas Territories	
	Georgia	
	Germany	
	Gibraltar	
City:		
State:	-- ⌄	
Contact First Name:		
Contact Last Name:		

This particular search returned 259 results, certainly enough to keep you busy for a while if you want agency clients in Germany. I would recommend doing this type of search for agencies in your source and target language country/countries. The ProZ Blue Board has similar search features you can use.

Again, as with translators' association directories, never use the contact information for an agency that you find in an agency rating service database. The site's terms of use may prohibit this, and the information may be outdated. Instead, go to the agency's website and use the application instructions that you find there.

3.3 Simple Google searches

A final option, especially if you already have a well-defined specialization, if you work in a hard-to-find language pair, or if your source or target language country does not have a translators' association that allows corporate members, is to do a simple Google search.

For example, you might search for "financial translation agency," or "translation agencies in Morocco," to find some agencies to apply to. This is particularly effective if you search by specialization, as you will find agencies that have a web page for your specializations (which is a good sign that they might need more translators in that specialization).

Chapter 4: Making contact

Now that you've prepared your translation-targeted resume and found quality agencies to apply to, it's time to start contacting those potential clients. For most agencies, this will be in one of two ways:

- Filling out application forms on the agency's website

- E-mailing the agency your resume

The first step is to go to the agency's website and find out their preferred application method. This is important: **do not circumvent the agency's preferred method**. For example, if the agency tells you to e-mail your resume in PDF format with your last name and non-English language in the filename, make sure you do that. If the agency asks you to fill out their online forms, do not try to "make an impression" by e-mailing it to them.

When you're on an agency's website, the best places to look for application instructions are obvious links such as "work with us," "join the team," "freelancers," "employment," etc. You can also try the Contact tab. Once you've found that, you'll know whether you should fill out the agency's application forms or e-mail them your resume. Here are some specific tips for each scenario.

4.1 If you are filling out a form
More and more agencies are streamlining their application process

by requiring you to fill out online forms with specific, required fields. Nearly every large agency now does this.

The downside is that these forms require you to provide certain information (such as specializations and rates) before you even have a conversation with the agency about their needs and your skills. Instead of being able to explain, "I do legal translation, especially legal documents with a financial component," or "I charge X cents per word, but for non-rush projects I may be able to charge Y cents per word," you simply have to fill in a form field.

When you fill out an agency's forms, *always* look for a place to include something personal. If there is a field for comments, "other information," etc., then paste the text of your cover e-mail into that box. Agencies use forms for a reason: they're easier to process and also cut down on spam applications. But they require that you go to a little more work in order to put any sort of personal touch on your application.

4.2 If you are applying by e-mail

Some agencies will ask that you e-mail them your resume. First, check if there are any particular requirements for the e-mail or your resume. Typical requirements include putting your language pairs or specializations in the subject line of your e-mail or in the filename of your resume. If the agency has special requirements, make sure that you follow them.

Next, write an engaging cover e-mail. The basic rules are the same as for your resume: keep it short, don't tell your life story, and hit the highlights first. Also, *always* put the agency's name in the first line of the e-mail, so that they can tell it is not being sent to thousands of potential clients at once. Here are a few examples of cover e-mails that you can use for inspiration.

From a translator with experience and a clear specialization:

"To the attention of [insert name of agency]. I am an Italian to English translator specializing in medical and pharmaceutical translation, and I recently came across your website while doing a search for high-quality agencies in the New York area. I am attaching my resume for your consideration. I have five years of experience as a full-time freelance translator, and my recent experience includes Italian to English translation of medical reports, clinical trial patient questionnaires, and patient information sheets. Please let me know if you need any more information from me, and I look forward to the opportunity of working together soon."

From a beginning translator:

"To the attention of [insert name of agency]. I am an English to Spanish translator, and recently came across your website while researching high-quality translation agencies in San Francisco. I recently launched my freelance translation business after completing a translation certificate from [name of school], and I am actively seeking agency clients. I am attaching my resume for your consideration, and I am available to take a translation test at your convenience. I appreciate your time and hope to collaborate with you soon."

Whether you apply to agencies via their forms or by e-mailing them, it's important to follow up until the agency sends you some work, assuming that they are interested in using your services. More on that in the next chapter.

Chapter 5: Following up

Once you've made your initial contact with an agency, they may respond right away to let you know the next step in their application process. Otherwise, you will need to follow up with them. It's helpful to have three "touch points" with every potential agency client:

1. Find the agency and apply to them.

2. If you receive *any* response from a human (meaning, not from an auto-responder), even "we aren't looking for new translators in your language pair right now, but we'll keep your materials on file," follow it up with a handwritten note. The note can be short: "Thank you very much for responding to my inquiry about English to Swedish translation opportunities with your company. I appreciate your time and look forward to working together in the future." Always include a business card. The goal here is simply to personalize the contact and show the agency that you're serious.

3. If you really want to stand out, send a handwritten note even if the agency doesn't respond. Try something like, "I recently applied for English to Japanese translation work via your website. Thank you for considering my application, and I hope to work together soon." Enclose a business card.

4. If you haven't heard from the agency in about a month, send a short follow-up e-mail just to make sure they still know that you're interested. Something like, "Thanks again for responding to my application about Norwegian to English translation work with your agency. I noticed it's been about a month since you received my application. I wondered if you need any more information from me, and I also wanted to reiterate my interest in working with you. Thank you for your time and consideration."

5.1 The hard truth about good agencies

Marketing to agencies can get discouraging. During my first year as a translator, I applied to over 400 agencies before I had enough clients to provide me with full-time work. And that was in 2002, when there were fewer freelancers and probably less competition than we see today. So, an agency marketing push can feel like a slog; that's the truth.

Here's another truth: if you want to work with higher-quality agencies, expect to be told that they don't need you right now, but will keep your materials on file in case they need you in the future. In general, high-quality agencies are not actively recruiting for translators. These agencies are many translators' most desirable clients; they combine many of the positive aspects of an agency (a steady flow of work, with the agency handling the non-translation work) with many of the positive aspects of a direct client (interesting projects and higher pay). Translators who land these kinds of agencies as clients tend to stick with them for a long time. As a result, you may, or probably will have to play the waiting game until one of the agency's regular translators leaves or is too busy for them, or until the agency itself gets a new client. Some high-quality agencies may have only a few regular translators per language combination.

The key here is to stay on that agency's radar screen, so that you're the person who comes to mind when they do need a new translator. If you drop off the radar screen after the initial contact, you're unlikely to get work from them. You need to keep following up every month or so. Take any chance you get to meet with that agency in person. Without being a pest, let them know that you're still interested, so that they remember you when they need to add a team member.

5.2 Pro tips for following up

You can follow up more often than you think, without being annoying. Part of your goal is to make a human connection, amid the many applications that agencies receive that are either a) spam or b) from unqualified translators. So, don't be afraid to follow up at least once a month. But make sure to mix it up. Don't just e-mail the agency and ask whether they have any work for you. Try techniques such as:

- Putting a Google Alert on the agency's name, so that you know what's going on with them. Use that information as a jumping-off point for your e-mails. "Congratulations on winning the local Chamber of Commerce Award." "I noticed that you hired a new project manager; congratulations on your growth!"

- Letting the agency know what you've been up to, in case they have similar needs. "I recently translated four annual reports, for companies in a variety of sectors. As annual report season continues, let me know if you need help with similar projects."

- Sending links to articles that might be helpful to the agency. If you want to get really ambitious, you could follow the local business news in their area. Let the agency know about potential clients, even if they wouldn't need your language pair. "I noticed that a German wind power company recently selected Raleigh for its North American headquarters. That struck me as potentially a good fit for your services if you're looking for new clients."

- Sending cards for the holidays, International Translation Day (September 30), and any holidays specific to your language or culture (Chinese New Year, etc.).

Chapter 6: Tracking your marketing efforts

Tracking your marketing efforts serves several purposes.

- You know who you've contacted, so that you don't contact the same agency twice.

- You know what stage each contact is at. Did the agency respond? Do you need to follow up with them at a specific interval ("We'll be looking for more financial translators when annual report season rolls around")? Did they mention anything else of note ("Let's try to meet for coffee at the ATA conference")?

- You can track your follow-up efforts.

- You know which agencies to eliminate from future follow-up or marketing efforts, for example agencies that pay half of your minimum rate.

- Tracking forces you to be honest about how many agencies you've contacted. Without that, it's easy to be overly optimistic about how many contacts you've made.

6.1 Tracking methods

Your tracking method is much less important than the fact that you do the tracking. Even a very simple tracking method like index cards can work, as long as you're scrupulous about putting information into it.

From least to most sophisticated, three potential tracking methods you might consider are:

- Paper (index cards or a notebook)

- A spreadsheet

- A contact management tool

Of these three, the method I recommend for most translators is a spreadsheet. It's easy to use, and you already have the software to implement it (usually Excel or Google Docs). Contact management software like Salesforce or Zoho can be really helpful as long as you don't spend more time managing the tool than it's worth. Beware of this phenomenon (not just with contact management software). It's easy to get drawn in by the idea of a specialized tool for each task, but in many cases a very simple option will work for a freelancer's needs.

If you'd like to start with a simple spreadsheet tracking method, just create a spreadsheet called something like "Contacts_begin_August1" (insert the date on which you're starting). Then create columns for the various items you want to track, like this:

	A	B	C	D	E
1	Date contacted	Agency	How contacted	Outcome	Followup
2	5/15/2017	XYZ translations	Applied on website	Responded-received	Sent card, 5/22
3					

At a minimum, I would recommend tracking the items listed above:

- Date you contacted the agency

- The agency's name

- How you contacted them: did you fill out their web application, e-mail them your resume, give them a paper resume at an in-person event, or something else?

- Outcome: what happened then? Did the agency acknowledge receipt of your application? Did they ask for more information, or for you to take a translation test?

- Followup: What followup steps have you taken? Did you send them a handwritten card? E-mail them to make sure they received your application?

6.2 How many contacts?

Part of the point of tracking your marketing efforts is to keep you honest about how many contacts you've made. When left to our own devices, most of us overestimate, and sometimes radically overestimate the number of marketing contacts we've made, or the return we should expect to see on those contacts.

Lots of translators wonder how many contacts they should make, or will need to make when marketing to agencies. And again, most people underestimate the number and overestimate the response rate. I get lots of e-mails from beginning translators, lamenting, "I've applied to 25 agencies and haven't gotten much of a response." And certainly, you'll talk to translators who never did a mass marketing campaign to agencies. They marketed in other ways: through friends who already worked in the industry, or through the local market, for example. But the majority of translators will do a mass marketing campaign to agencies at some point.

Like it or not, marketing to agencies is cold selling; you're approaching clients you don't know and who don't know you, and making a pitch for your services. When I started my freelance business in 2002, I applied to over 400 agencies during my first year in business, and it still took about a year and a half until I was replacing the income from my previous full-time job. As in any other type of cold selling, you should expect a response rate of about 1%-3%, so about one to three new clients for every 100 clients you contact. That being said:

- Luck enters into the equation as well; you may get lucky and hit an agency that just happens to have landed a big new client that requires your languages or specializations.

- The success rate will definitely depend on your languages and specializations. A generalist English to Spanish translator in the US is going to have to work a lot harder than a Japanese to English financial translator living in Japan.

The real answer to the "how many contacts" question is either comforting or discouraging, depending on how you look at it: until you have enough work. One key quality of successful beginning freelance translators is a willingness to market as much as is needed to develop a viable business. The successful beginners are the ones who say, "I'm planning to work 40 hours a week, and if I don't have any work that week, then I market for 40 hours." Rather than taking free time when they don't have paying work, those ultra-motivated freelancers use every available moment to market when they don't have as much work as they want. And, not surprisingly, they're the ones who, pretty soon, do have as much work as they want.

In real terms, most beginning freelancers need to count on six months to a year of very spotty work volumes, then probably another six months to a year until they are spending most of their time working instead of looking for work. One exception to this is translators who immediately go to work for large agencies; I recently talked to a brand-new freelancer who sent out one resume to a very large agency, was immediately hired, and started working for that agency nearly full-time. That's an option. But otherwise, about the fastest I've seen a new freelancer develop a base of regular clients is about six months. Bottom line: take the long view, keep marketing until you have as much work as you want, and give yourself six months to a year until your workflow really starts to pick up.

Chapter 7: Don't ignore the local market

Translators can and do work with clients all over the world; that's one of the great things about our job and our industry. But amid your excitement about working with clients anywhere, don't forget the local market. Those personal connections still matter. When I started my freelance business, I asked for an informational interview with every agency in my local area; even if the agency said that they didn't need more translators for my languages, I went anyway. And many of those agencies ended up eventually sending me work; a far greater success rate than from my online-only contacts.

If you'd like to do some in-person marketing in your local area, first identify a few potential clients. You can also use the "local area" technique in other places; for example if you're going on vacation to another major city, you could use this technique there.

Once you've identified the potential clients, think of a hook; a way to create a connection that gives you the opportunity to suggest a meeting with them. Being a member of the same local association is always a good hook, such as, "I'm a member of the Elvish Translators Association and came across your listing in the online directory. I wonder if I might drop by your offices for a short meeting at a time that's convenient for you, to learn a little more about your business and how I might fit in."

Many small to medium-sized agencies will be interested in this sort of thing, because it allows them to widen their pool of translators, and livens up their work day (especially if they work in an office with just a few people). Over the years, our industry has lost a lot of the personal connections that many people really enjoy, so this request for an informational interview is worth a try.

Then, you'll need to think about what to ask the potential client when you meet with them. The key here is to:

- Avoid being overly self-promotional. The potential client knows that your real reason for meeting with them is to hopefully get some work. You don't need to belabor that point.

- Honestly use the meeting as an opportunity to gather useful information, without prying into the client's confidential information. So, you could ask questions such as:

  o How long has the agency been in business?

  o Have they always been located in your area?

  o What are the main language pairs or specializations that they handle?

  o What languages are the hardest to find translators for?

  o What are their growth areas?

  o Are they a member of any associations that they would recommend that you join?

  o Do they provide services other than translation, like transcription, multilingual DTP, subtitling, etc.?

You want to avoid prying into the specifics of who the agency works for. Never ask direct questions like, "Who are your major clients?" or "Do you work with X end client?" or "Does X translator work for you?" or "What rates do you charge end clients?" Try to keep the meeting to around 20 minutes, and at the end, leave the agency a business card and a resume, and perhaps a small gift to thank them for their time. Write a handwritten followup note to the person who met with you.

Other sources of potential local clients include:

- International chambers of commerce

- World Trade associations

- Country-specific chambers of commerce (German-American Chamber of Commerce, Scandinavian Chamber of Commerce, etc.)

- Country or language-specific business associations (French-American Business Association, etc.)

Chapter 8: What about online marketplaces?

Online marketplaces like Upwork, ProZ, TranslatorsCafe, etc. have pluses and minuses. On the plus side:

- Clients who post translation projects on job-boards are "pre-sold." They already know that they need a translator, and are ready to get going as soon as they find the right person.

- There are tons of jobs out there looking for translators. Just go on the online marketplaces and start looking.

- Online marketplaces can be a good source of long-term, well-paying clients, if you do a difficult-to-find language pair or specialization, or if you use them to look for work at times when other translators are not usually working (i.e. the week between Christmas and January 1 in the US).

However, these marketplaces also have a lot of downsides:

- The "reverse auction" phenomenon, where the cheapest, fastest translators get selected for most projects.

- Clients getting swamped with bids from so many translators that they can never evaluate them all, usually resulting in the client selecting the fastest or cheapest person.

- An ever-faster race to the bottom, where rates for saturated language pairs (i.e. English to Spanish) may be so low that it's difficult to make a living.

My advice is to approach job boards with caution. If you do a hard-to-find language combination or specialization, you may want to have a profile on these types of sites, and bid on jobs advertised there. If you do a more common language, job boards can be a decent starting point, but the key (as with most huge agencies) is not to get stuck there. It's one thing for a complete beginner translator to say, "I'm going to hit the job boards to find two or three projects that I can use as resume-builders and references." It's another thing to have the vast majority of your work coming from job boards when you can, and should be, moving up to better work. If you'd like to use job boards, follow a few guidelines:

- Emphasize quality to the extent that you can. Do not use words like "inexpensive," "affordable," "budget-friendly," etc. in your profile. Instead, capitalize on the fact that many clients have been burned by terrible translations that they procured from job boards. Emphasize that you get the job done right the first time, you don't outsource it to anyone else, you don't use Google Translate, you follow the client's instructions to the letter, and so on.

- Be honest about the fact that you're not cheap. I think it's perfectly acceptable to say to a job board client, "I'm sure that you'll get lower bids, but I want to emphasize that I'm a full-time professional translator. I guarantee a prompt response to your phone calls and e-mails, and I follow your instructions to the letter, with the project delivered on or before the deadline." This is likely to differentiate you from the average "lifer" job board translator.

- Negotiate concessions other than price. Can the client extend the deadline? Can they have one of their staff do some of the formatting? Can they provide you with an editable file rather than a PDF?

- Don't get stuck. If you are earning sub-optimal rates through job board clients, use them only as a springboard. Identify clients like your job board clients, but who are less price-sensitive, and start applying to them right away.

- Don't completely ignore job boards as sources of good clients. There is definitely some wheat among the chaff if you look hard enough, and for long enough. Many clients post projects on job boards because they don't know where else to look, or because they've never worked with a translator before and find the job board through a Google search. So, don't be immediately suspicious of every client you find on a job board, just be selective in how and why you use these online marketplaces.

Chapter 9: Rate negotiations and test translations

Agency rate negotiations can be tricky, and rates are a source of fear for a lot of translators. Many translators get caught in this kind of trap: "I'm afraid that if I set my rates too high, I won't have enough work. And if I set them too low, I'll be working really long hours just to meet my basic expenses." And there's some truth to those fears.

- Your main consideration when setting your rates should be how much you need or want to earn, not fear of losing out on work, or vague speculation about what the client will pay.

- Many freelancers think that by pricing their work on the low end, they'll find more clients and more work. But low rates can be a very negative signal to quality-conscious clients: the client thinks either "This person has very little confidence in their work," or "This person has very little business sense," or both. When clients see a translator whose rates are at the high end, they are more likely to think, "This person's work is probably very good, so they charge what the market will bear for it."

- In the agency world, you can only compete on quality to a certain extent. I don't mean this as a negative statement, just a realistic one. Whereas some direct clients will say, "Whatever it costs to get a great translation, we'll pay it," agencies generally have a fairly narrow rate range for each language pair, and you must fall within that rate range if you want to work with them.

- Some agencies will require you to enter your rates on their online application, with no rate range: just "I charge X for translation, X for editing," etc. Personally I think those agencies are prioritizing efficiency over any sort of personal relationship with their translators, but that's their choice. If that happens, you really have no choice but to enter the rate that is acceptable to you.

- If the agency doesn't require you to enter your rates in the application, then you have a little more wiggle room. Inevitably, the agency will ask what you charge. I would recommend against giving a range; the problem is that if you say "between X and Y cents per word," the client will tend to focus on the low end, while you will tend to focus on the high end. I find it more effective to give one number, but with some wiggle room, like, "My standard rate is X cents per word, but if that's not in your budget, let me know and we can discuss it further." You're not saying, "I'll give a discount," you're just saying that you're willing to discuss it.

9.1 When clients ask for discounts

In an ideal world, you and the client have a bilateral negotiation about your rates, and the client takes other factors into consideration: the demand for your languages and specializations, how much they anticipate needing you, your level of experience, certifications, etc. But sometimes, a potential agency client will unilaterally say, "Our maximum rate for your language pair is X," and it's up to you to accept or decline. Here are a few considerations in that situation:

- Most importantly, how much do you need or want this work? Are you going to resent this client if you say yes? Would you be better off saying no and using that time to market to other, better-paying clients?

- If you are being paid by the word, how time-intensive is this work likely to be? It's important to focus not just on the per-word rate, but on your projected hourly rate when you work for this client.

- A client never *makes you* lower your rates. They ask, and you agree or don't. I hear way too many translators who say, "That agency made me give a discount." (No, they didn't). The choice is always up to you.

- Are there any non-economic reasons for working with this client? Is their work particularly interesting? Do they pay quickly? Do they have work in a specialization you're looking to break into?

- How close are you to reaching your target work volume or target income? I find that a lot of translators get unnecessarily stressed about turning work down or declining to give discounts, even when they have as much work as they want, and are earning what they want to earn. This makes no sense. If you don't really need this client's work, why agree to a discounted rate?

- Have a "red zone" rate, which you never go below, no matter what. I recommend that every translator has three rate zones: green (ideal), yellow (not ideal, but acceptable under certain circumstances), and red (no way). Force yourself to stick to that red zone rate: never work for less than that number, under any circumstances.

9.2 Translation tests

Many agencies will ask you to take a translation test before working with them. Whether or not to accept depends on (say it with me now…) how much you need or want the client's work. Agencies may require that you take an unpaid test, end of story. It's up to you whether to accept, but if you decline, you will not be considered for work with that agency. Sample translations tend not to carry much weight with agencies, because they prefer to compare all of their prospective translators' work on the same sample, in order to assess typical mistranslations and style difficulties.

It's always worth asking to be paid for a test translation; the worst the agency can say is "no," and then you can still decline to take the test if you want. I have mixed feelings about unpaid tests:

- In one sense, translators are not the only professionals who are ever asked for this type of thing. When I hire a new accountant or web designer for my business, my assumption is that they offer some type of free consultation to talk about what I need and whether they're a good fit. Let's say this usually lasts 15-30 minutes; shorter than most test translations take, but it's still something. Additionally, tests allow agencies to compare multiple translators' work on the same passage; they can also pick a passage that closely resembles the work that they typically need translators in that language combination/specialization to do.

- In another sense, unpaid test translations can feel exploitative. Even at 250 words or so, the unpaid test will take most translators about an hour including proofreading, and most often, the only feedback from the agency is "you passed," or "you failed." Translators (understandably) get frustrated when they pass an agency's unpaid test, only to get no work from that agency for months.

Unpaid tests are a real balancing act, and ultimately come down to how much you need or want that particular client's work. I also think that agencies are smart to simply start promising new translators on small projects, in order to see how they perform in real-world situations rather than in a fairly artificial test environment (for example, with no time limits).

Chapter 10: The changing realities of the agency market

The agency market has changed a lot in the 15 years I've been freelancing. I do think that translators can still be successful when working primarily or exclusively with agency clients, but I would say that:

- Working with many agencies, especially large ones, is now a fairly impersonal and transactional process. There's much more downward rate pressure than when I started in the agency market, and some of the agencies I started with 15 years ago now pay *less* than what they paid back then. Many of the larger agencies don't cultivate or really even want a personal relationship with their translators; they just want to know if you can take on the work that they need done, starting right now. Under those circumstances, it's understandable that many translators start to feel like cogs in the machine.

- It's hard to make a living on low-end agency rates. At the lower end of the agency market, volumes are high and rates are low, requiring translators to set relatively low financial goals, translate very high volumes of text, or both.

- As more people enter the freelance market, higher-end agencies have less of an incentive to work with beginners. It's now common to see agencies simply say—at least for the more common language pairs—that they do not accept applications from translators with less than three years' experience, or without some type of certification. This is because these agencies receive so many unsolicited applications that they can afford to be choosy.

- Higher-end agencies—the ones most translators want to work with—are often fully staffed and not actively looking for translators, unless you do a difficult-to-find language pair or specialization. You'll probably need to wait until one of their regular translators leaves, or the agency itself gets a new client, until you obtain work from them.

- Many agencies require the use of specific translation tools such as translation memory software, machine translation plugins, quality-checking software such as XBench, etc. Many agencies that require these tools also impose translation memory discounts, requiring you to charge less than 100% of your per-word rate, depending on the match percentage of the segment that you're translating.

This is not to say that the agency market is all bad, or is to be avoided. But it's important to be realistic about the agency market's challenges before you dive in!

Questions from readers

Thank you very much to the readers of my blog, Thoughts on Translation, for submitting the questions that appear in this chapter. Some of them have given me permission to use their names and some preferred to remain anonymous.

Question: *When I first started out as a freelance translator, I became a member of ProZ.com and waited for postings to come up that I would like to work on and met my financial goals. However, as I became more specialized this endeavor became more frustrating because the agencies posting on that website were not willing to pay what I needed to earn in order to make a decent living. How do we go about targeting the right agencies to work for given our specialties and financial objectives? —Rose Tello*

Answer: A couple of options here:

- Do a simple Google search (i.e. "medical translation agency").

- Search on Payment Practices or the ProZ Blue Board for agencies with your specialization in their name.

- Ask for referrals from translators who work in your specializations but in other language pairs—so that it doesn't look as if you're trying to poach their clients.

- Actively pursue local agencies that you can meet with in person.

- Actively network at translation industry conferences such as the ATA conference where you can meet agencies in person.

Once you move up in the translation market, you also have to accept that many, or perhaps even most agencies may not want to pay your desired rates. That's OK: you've completed the important step of calculating what you need or want to earn, and you don't need hundreds of clients who will pay your desired rates. You need only enough clients for you to achieve your desired monthly or yearly income.

Question:

1. *Is there any way to convince a translation agency whose requirements include three years' experience in the translation industry to work with you even though you only have one year of experience in translation but many more in a key sector (like finance for instance)?*

2. *How do you go about raising your rates with an agency you have been working with for over a year?*

3. *What can you possibly do when, after taking a test, the agency tells you that you have failed when in fact their proofreader has introduced errors where they were not? —Karine Derancy*

Answers:

1. I would recommend addressing this on an individual basis with the agency. Definitely do not just circumvent their requirements: if they say "three years' experience required," do not just submit

your application as if you are not subject to that requirement. I think the best option would be to send them an e-mail, such as, "I noticed on your website that you require three years' experience in order to apply for freelance translation work. Although I have only been translating for a year, I have X years of experience in the financial sector, including X, Y, and Z roles and skills, which I apply in my financial translation work. Would this make me eligible to apply for freelance work with your agency now?"

2. The best time to negotiate for a higher rate is before you ever work for the agency, and preferably when you're not desperate for their work. That gives you the freedom to walk away if the agency won't pay your rates. Once you're working for the agency, you have a few options, depending on how much you need or want their work:

- "As of August 1, my base rate will change to X cents per word. I very much appreciate your business, and in order to save your time and mine, please contact me only for projects for which this rate is in your budget." That gets the point across, but it also tells the agency that if they cannot pay your higher rate, you're not interested in working with them anymore.

- "In reviewing my accounting for last year, I noticed that the rate I've been charging you since X date is now significantly lower than the rates that my other agency clients pay. I really enjoy working with you and very much appreciate your business. However, I find it necessary to increase my rate to the average rate paid by my other agency clients, which is X. I will continue charging my current rate until X date, after which my new rate will take effect." This achieves a similar effect, but with a little more explanation.

- "In reviewing my accounting for last year, I noticed that the rate I've been charging you since X date is now significantly lower than the rates that my other agency clients pay. Would it be possible to talk about the potential impact on my workflow from you if I were to raise my rate to X cents per word?" This could be seen as an "exploratory" e-mail to see if the client will pay more, but it also feels a bit tentative, which isn't the impression you want to give the client.

3. Failing an agency's test is never fun. You can certainly try—politely—to point out the errors that were introduced. However, many agencies don't want to negotiate about test results: if the person who evaluated your test says that you failed, the agency is unlikely to reconsider. Personally, I would simply move on, since your relationship with the agency is unlikely to improve after this experience. But if you want to pursue it with them, I think it's worth one carefully-worded e-mail.

Question: *I'm wondering how to find and market to smaller boutique agencies? —Anton Filinov*

Answer: This is a tricky one, because a lot of these agencies are less visible—online, in conference exhibit halls—than larger agencies are. In addition, as I mentioned above, smaller boutique agencies use fewer translators and are thus less likely to be actively recruiting new translators. So you may have to follow up with them multiple times and play a bit of a waiting game until they need you. That being said, I would recommend trying:

- In-person contacts with agencies in your area.

- Referrals from translators who work in other language pairs.

- Mentioning on your website, LinkedIn profile, etc. that you prefer working with smaller, boutique agencies.

- Raising your own profile by writing for translation industry publications, presenting at conferences, etc.

Question:

1. *How should you proceed when your longest-standing agency client says they can't raise your rates and you still want to work with them because you value the projects they send you as well as their timely payment practices?*

2. *If an agency client pushes you to take on a project you've already kindly declined, how should you reply so as to sound determined but not blatant? Should you sound blatant? —Anonymous*

Answers:

1. This situation presents a dilemma for a lot of freelancers; it's also a rationale for not being overly dependent on one client. In an ideal world, you would simply set a minimum rate below which you do not go, and then decline to work with any client who doesn't meet that rate. In the real world, there are non-financial considerations that come into play, including the ones that you mention here. Additionally, the agency has been clear about their position: they can't or won't pay more, and it's up to you to decide what to do with that information. You could:

- Simply stop working with them if they won't pay your minimum rate.

- Continue working with them for the moment while you look for higher-paying clients.

- Set a quota of work that you will do for them every month, and don't go above that quota.

- Live with the fact that they won't pay your minimum rate, and accept that you enjoy working with them for other reasons.

There's no perfect solution here, other than finding a better-paying client to replace this one.

2. Some agencies will ask more than once whether you can take on a project, and you can't blame them for trying. I think that you have two options:

- Politely but firmly decline: "Unfortunately I have to decline; I really can't take this on."

- Explain the circumstances which could allow you to accept: "I could take this on if you could extend the deadline by two days." "I could take this on if a rush rate is in your budget." And then it's on the agency to agree or not.

Question: *As I struggle with the constant downward pressure on rates from agencies that deal with my specialization, I'm looking to broaden my field of work to include areas that I used to work in when just starting out, but am less specialized in. Do you have any suggestions on how to parlay my existing agency contacts for work in areas I have put aside, so I can increase my specialization in those? To be specific, I have a certificate in legal translation and I have also translated general mechanical engineering and environmental impact studies, RFPs, etc. —Anne Louise*

Answer: A couple of thoughts here. First, the areas that you mention are technical and demanding; not something you want to launch yourself into if you feel tentative. So my first suggestion would be that you need to move your skills from "…less specialized in" to a higher level. Take some Coursera courses; pay an experienced translator to mentor you in those areas or have you re-translate their old translations as practice assignments, until you feel really confident in your abilities. Then, you have a platform from which to approach your existing contacts. "I've recently honed my expertise in (mechanical engineering translation, for example) by taking several online courses in mechanical engineering, attending a mechanical engineers' conference, and doing multiple skill development sessions with an experienced mechanical engineering translator. I have added mechanical engineering to my list of specializations, so please keep me in mind should you have any assignments in my language pair."

Question: *The majority of translation agencies look for the freelancers with the lowest rates and fastest delivery time, sometimes at the cost of quality. Naturally, they aim to profit as much as they possibly can. How would you describe your dream translation agency to work with and what requirements should be met for you to even consider translating for the agency, since you may be well equipped to find your own clients and customers —Siret Entson*

Answer: This is definitely a consideration for more experienced translators. These days, if I get an "out of the blue" inquiry from an agency, the chances are extremely high that they will not pay my rates, and that they may be offering perhaps half of my minimum rate. However, I do still work with agencies, and I enjoy the agencies that I work with.

My dream agency:

- Has an inside line to end clients that would be difficult for me to work with as an individual freelancer, most often because they have a sporadic need for large volumes of work, or because they need many languages and don't want to work with individual freelancers.

- Insulates me from "end-client drama." They handle all of the non-translation aspects of the work, so that I just translate.

- Puts me in touch with the other translators working on the projects I work on, so that we can collaborate.

- Does not haggle about rates for individual projects. I have a set rate that I always charge them, and our mutual understanding is that when they contact me for a project, they are willing to pay that rate.

My longstanding agency clients fit that profile, and I enjoy working with them just as much as with my direct clients.

Question: *Many translation agencies ask me to take an unpaid test, although I am already certified, and when I tell the agencies that I would prefer to provide samples of my relevant previous work, they reject the offer. Is undertaking the free tests considered to be a real marketing tool to gain more clients, meaning that we as freelance translators should take the risk? How can we avoid this? Or at least how can we persuade clients that the free test does not reflect the real abilities of a good translator.- Carolina Cortez, Dolores Guinazu and Hani Hassaan*

Answer: Unpaid tests are a tricky topic. When people say that other professionals do not do free work in exchange for the promise of paid work, I actually disagree. When I hire a new web designer, accountant, etc., it's actually the norm—at least where I live—that the person offers a free consultation to determine if we're a good fit. In my experience, agencies are unlikely to accept samples of your past work instead of a test, perhaps/probably because they want to compare your work to the work of other translators who have also translated that test—the agency knows where the pitfalls and tricky parts are, and they want to see how you handle them. It's also the norm that agencies will not give you any detailed feedback on your test; they will simply tell you whether you passed or failed. Presumably that's because they don't want to arbitrate an argument between you and the person who evaluated the test. If unpaid tests really bother you, don't take them. Look for clients that don't require them. It's also worth offering the agency an alternative. Try telling them that you don't take tests because you feel that they don't reflect how you work under actual conditions (for example, a deadline!). Suggest that the agency start you out on a minimum-charge job instead. If you do choose to take unpaid tests, I would recommend:

- Limiting the test to about 250 words. That's enough for the agency to get a sense of your skills, and should not take you more than about 45 minutes, no matter how carefully you go over your work.

- Discussing rates and demand before you take the test. "In order to take your unpaid test, I would first need to confirm that my minimum rate of X cents per word is within the range of rates that you pay for my language pair, and that you either have or anticipate a need for additional translators in my language pair, such that I would begin receiving work from you soon after taking the test, assuming that I pass it." I do think it's important to talk about rates up front—it saves your time and the agency's—and to specify that you do not take tests just to be added to a long list of translators who may or may not get work from that agency.

Question: *Do you have any thoughts or recommendations for translators on the use of platforms such as Fiverr, etc.—which aren't actually translation agencies, but rather, platforms for seeking diverse freelance work opportunities—to get translation work? —Dan Villarreal*

Answer: These types of online platforms (Fiverr, Upwork, etc.) can be either great or horrible, depending on what you find. In one sense, it's unrealistic to look for work on a site like Fiverr and be surprised that you find only low-end work there. Someone who looks for a translator on a site whose marketing pitch is "Everything $5!" is not likely to be a premium client. On the other hand, when a client who knows nothing about translation has to find a translator, they are likely to look in the same place they would look for any other type of service provider: Fiverr, Upwork, Thumbtack, even Craigslist. So there could be some wheat among the chaff. My suggestion would be to focus on sites like Upwork where you name your price and clients see it displayed on your profile. For example when I wanted to expand the content marketing writing side of my business, I posted a profile on Upwork, clearly listing a rate of $90 an hour. This resulted in some excellent clients who were not looking for a $5 solution.

Question: *What do you do when you have been translating for over four years for a well-known translation agency with great success. They rate you more than once as "excellent" and "very satisfied" in the ProZ WWA (Willingness to Work Again) program and send you complimentary remarks after the translation delivery. You decide once to mention the successful work you do with them (without mentioning their clients' names* *or trademarks or translation confidential content) in your portfolio. They contact you forbidding you to mention you work for them, and when you ask why not, they escalate this discussion from the PM to the executive management. The next day you are simply informed by e-mail that they no longer need your translation services because they have enough translators in your language pairs (in my case two language pairs!). —Anonymous*

Answer: Clients can be funny that way! All joking aside, I always tell the students in my classes that the safest option is to **never** mention a client's name unless you have their permission in writing. Honestly, who knows what the client's objection is? If they enjoy working with you, it certainly doesn't seem that their reputation is going to be tarnished by a public mention of your relationship with them. But in the end, the client pays the bills—in the form of your invoices, and by association, your living expenses and household bills. So I would take the safe option and never mention specific clients by name unless you've asked them in writing and they've agreed.

Question: *I work with Brazilian Portuguese as a target language but do not live in Brazil; I live in Europe. The difference between the euro and the Brazilian currency is huge: 1 euro = 3.3 BR Real. European translation agencies contacting me for BR Portuguese jobs then expect me to charge the same (lower) rate per word (due to the weaker currency) charged in Brazil by local Brazilian translators, despite the fact that I live in Europe under another (stronger) currency, and where all EU translators charge an average rate three times higher than Brazilians do. How can I make a living under this misconceived (but quite convenient for the client) reasoning? —Anonymous*

Answer: Brazilian Portuguese is definitely not the only language to be affected by this phenomenon; I'd venture a guess that Spanish, Russian, and the majority of the Eastern European languages have been hit hard by it as well. Option #1 – undoing the Internet and preventing clients from accessing translators in countries with lower costs of living or lower prevailing translation rates—probably isn't going to work. I would recommend:

- Being honest with clients: you can't afford to charge what in-country translators in Brazil charge, because you live in a country with a higher cost of living. If clients are looking for rock-bottom rates, that's not your target market.

- Being honest with yourself: you can't compete with the rates that in-country translators in Brazil charge, because you live in a country with a higher cost of living.

- Aggressively looking for clients in higher-paying countries. For example, agencies in Switzerland might have a need for into-Portuguese translators due to all of the international organizations there. In the end, I think this is the only real solution: trying to squeeze Eurozone rates out of agencies looking for Brazilian rates is likely to lead to intense frustration for you and the agencies.

Question: *With my specialization (pharmaceuticals and medicine), it is difficult to find direct clients, as they are usually huge companies with large-scale translation projects (too large for one translator). So, I work with agencies, and it is OK for me. But one of the problems when working with agencies is the difficulty in receiving testimonials. Most of them just refuse to give any publicly-available feedback. I guess it is because of some commercial considerations (competition and so on). But what can we do? Clients' recommendations are so important in our business! Without testimonials, a translator working with agencies looks inferior to a translator working with direct clients: we just have no evidence of our* *successful working relationships. —Tatyana Nikitina and Rachael Koev*

Answer: This is definitely an issue, especially when you want to break out of the marketing pitch that 99% of translators write about themselves, i.e. "I'm fast, accurate, and reliable!" Something a client says about you is so much more powerful than what you say about yourself. A couple of options:

- Search your old e-mails for positive comments from agency clients, and use them anonymously. "Thanks for your great work on this project; the client was really happy with it."— Translation agency project manager.

- Send your agency clients a customer satisfaction survey. Again, this would have to be anonymous, but you could set something up on Survey Monkey really easily, with just a couple of questions: "On a scale of 1-5, how happy were you with my translation services?" "On a scale of 1-5, how likely would you be to work with me again, or to recommend me to a colleague or friend?" "Would you like to offer any comments on my work?" That should result in some feedback that you could use anonymously.

- Ask your agency clients to write a recommendation on your LinkedIn profile. That way, it's not awkward if they decline, and some might accept. The advantage there is that their name is then out in public, and you can safely use the testimonial without fear that it's confidential.

Question: *When applying to agencies, how do I determine my "translation agency" rate per word? How can I stay away from being too low or too high? My language pair is English< >Spanish. —Beverly Hayes*

Answer: Most translators base their rate decisions on:

- Vague speculation about what other people are charging or what the market will bear

- Fear of pricing themselves too high and not having enough work

Instead, try this: first, figure out how much you need or want to earn. How much money do you want in your bank account every month? Add to that all of your business expenses: taxes, health insurance, paid vacation, retirement account contributions, professional development, computer hardware and software, professional association memberships, office supplies and equipment, any services you hire (accounting, web design, etc.), and so on. That's going to be a big number, but make your peace with it. Then, figure out how many hours per year you can or want to work. Take your desired working hours per week, multiply that by your desired working weeks per year, and subtract vacation time, holidays, sick days, etc. Divide your required gross income by your working hours per year, and you've got your required hourly rate. Divide that by your average translation speed, and you've got your required per-word rate. Then look for clients who will pay that rate. That's a better way to go about it.

The point here is that there are clients at *all* ranges of the rate spectrum. And the worst situation as a freelancer is to be working like crazy and still not making enough money. At least divide your rates into zones: green (a rate at which you are always happy to work), yellow (a rate at which you sometimes, but not always work) and red (a rate below which you never work). That's a much better option than applying to agencies and seeing what they're willing to pay you.

Question: *What should I do about including references on my* *translation-targeted resumé/CV? I translate from German to French, and—infrequently—from French to German or from Kirundi to German. I've been working primarily with three organizations for the past fifteen years. Do I have to ask them for written permission to publicly say that I work with them? I have the same question about using my German-language students as references. —Hermenegilde Ntabiriho*

Answer: As I mentioned in a previous response, the only safe options when it comes to references and testimonials are:

- Get the client or student's permission in writing

- Make the reference or testimonial anonymous

The point here is that the client has upheld their end of the deal by paying you for the work that you did for them. They're not obligated to let you use their name, and it's not really your business why they might not want to have their name used—always ask.

Question: *How do I deal with translation agencies that I don't want to work with anymore? I have been a freelance translator for 1.5 years now and at the beginning of my freelance career I applied to—literally—hundreds of agencies. Now I have a solid client base (only agencies so far) that I really enjoy working with. However, since I have applied to so many agencies, I regularly receive inquiries from agencies, that I actually don't want to work with anymore, since they have a way of working that I don't like (impersonal or mass mails: "Dear translator" or "Sorry for the mass mail, but this is a very urgent project." Should I keep them in my contacts just in case my regular clients don't have work for me anymore, or should I contact them directly to ask them to delete my data from their system? And if so, how do I phrase the e-mail in a professional and polite way? —Mandy Borchardt*

Answer: First and most importantly, congratulations on having a solid base of regular clients after only a year and a half of freelancing! Now, on to your dilemma, which is a good one for a freelancer to have. I recommend:

- For agencies whose relationship with you is so impersonal that you don't need to respond to their inquiries, just do nothing. If the required effort on your part is only to delete their e-mails for projects you don't want, it doesn't seem imperative to terminate the relationship, and you can always keep them as back-burner clients in the event that your regular clients don't have much work for you.

- If you are irritated by the e-mails themselves—and those "Apologies for the mass e-mail" messages can be a bit soul-crushing—then it's time to pull the Band-Aid off. You could try one of two strategies: ask the agency to cultivate a more personal relationship with you, or simply tell them that you want to be removed from their roster. If you think there's some hope of a more satisfying relationship with that client, then something like this could work. "Thank you so much for all of the offers of work that you've sent my way in recent months. Due to the volume of work that I have from my regular clients, I do not often respond to mass e-mails, or to offers of projects that are not directed specifically to me. However, I am very interested in working with you if you have projects that are assigned directly, rather than by mass e-mail." If you'd rather just cut the cord, something like this. "Thank you so much for all of the offers of work that you've sent my way in recent months. Due to the volume of work that I have from my regular clients, I would like to be removed from your roster of available translators, to save your time and mine. Thanks and let me know if you need any more information from me in order to deactivate my profile."

Question: *Are there any good translation agency directories out there? I have found one online that contains hundreds of agencies, but only about a third of the agencies listed are worth the time spent applying to them. The others don't even have a professional website and the rates they are asking for are just laughable. It ends up being a waste of time. Any suggestions? —Sophie Roulland*

Answer: My favorite way to find agencies is Payment Practices (paymentpractices.net). That is not an affiliate deal. A membership is no more than $20 per year, and you can use it in a couple of ways: to find out what translators say about working with a particular agency, or to proactively search for good agencies to apply to.

Question: *In your opinion, what elements distinguish a "good" from a "bad" agency? Is it the rates, the deadlines, the quality of the PMs? What are the best practices that good agencies share? —Paolo Dagonnier*

Answer: This is partly a matter of your own preferences—mass e-mails ("Dear translators…") drive me crazy, but some translators really like them because they don't demand a response if you don't want the project. Some translators really want a personal relationship with their clients, while others don't really care; they'd rather just sit at their desks and translate. I do think that most translators are going to be reluctant to work for an agency that is very low-paying, doesn't pay on time, or treats them poorly. Personally, I prefer working for agencies where I don't have to haggle over rates for individual projects—meaning that when the agency contacts me, it means that they will pay my base rate. I also enjoy being put in touch with the other translators I'm working with on a project, and I enjoy working with agencies who make a good-faith effort to get answers from the end client when I have questions. But to me, those factors are somewhat secondary to having a client who pays my rates without haggling, pays on time, and treats me as a professional.

Question: *I would love to know how to make my agency application stand out from the crowd (besides the basics of correct spelling and including all the necessary information in my resume). Can I do this with some creative writing, for example by stepping out of the typical "language combo, specialization" email format? By calling them to see what they're looking for? —Molly Yurick and Erin Woodard*

Answer: In theory, I like the idea of getting a little creative. However, you're also faced with the fact that agencies need to (quickly) scan your information in a fairly standardized format, and they're looking for things like your language combination and specialization. Many agencies may search their resume database using keywords ("German to English pharmaceutical"), and you want to work within that paradigm as well. But I do like the idea of calling or e-mailing the agency to see what they're looking for (i.e. what are their most in-demand specializations in your language pair?) before you apply. I also like the idea of sending the agency your standard one or two-page agency resume *and* a more creatively written one-page profile as you might use for direct clients. I would not replace the resume with the one-page profile, but sending both of them might be an option worth considering.

Question: *As a relatively newbie translator, I would like to know how to react when the "negotiations" with agencies are one-way negotiations? I often get contacted by agencies who seem interested in working with me. We begin talking and they state that they want me to lower my rates, or use this specific machine translation tool, or this or that. I answer as tactfully as possible and make sure that they understand that I am open to negotiations but that I want compensation when I agree to one of their demands... and usually, they just stand their ground and want me to make all the effort. So I end up refusing to work in these conditions and being frustrated because there is no possible discussion. How can I negotiate more efficiently with agencies? —Sophie Vallery*

Answer: I think you've made a very realistic assessment of the situation: you can't change the agency's demands, so you have to decide whether or not you're willing to change your expectations. I do think that this kind of behavior is short-sighted on the part of the agencies. They're reducing their translators to a transactional commodity, rather than treating them as skilled and trained professionals who need to be evaluated as individuals. Agencies with inflexible requirements in terms of rates, software, etc., are undoubtedly excluding good translators who don't want to comply with those requirements. But the bottom line is, that's the agency's choice. If they feel that those requirements aren't preventing them from finding translators who produce translations that their end clients are really happy with, then they're unlikely to change. In that case, the only thing you can do is make your point to the agency in a straightforward but diplomatic way, as you mention here ("I'm eager to work with you, but at this time I'm unable to lower my rates"). If the agency won't budge, then it's up to you to decide how much you need or want their work.

Question: *I mainly work for direct clients, but I have been trying to work with agencies as well in order to have a more constant workflow* *when direct clients seem to "disappear." Nevertheless, I have noticed the rates of many translation agencies are pretty low, and it is quite tough to find agencies offering medium-"high" rates. In specializations like mine (one of which is surfing), you have these huge sports corporations (for instance) working through agencies as far as translation services are concerned (easier to deal with a certain number of foreign languages all at once) and the agencies apply the above-mentioned rates. The question is: is it a good working strategy to have, let's say, two or three medium-low-paying agencies with a pretty constant workflow, even though you do not get what you usually would or is it better to refuse working with them and concentrate on higher-paying clients? And, where are the fair-paying agencies? I personally like the tasks I am given (e.g. related to surfing), and I like working with them and this leads to an improvement of my skills in the fields I work with. Nevertheless I still have this doubt haunting me. —Martina Lunardelli*

Answer: You make some good points about the pluses and minuses of working with agencies; it's definitely true that some—but not all—large companies that need multiple languages are not inclined to work with freelancers. In terms of whether you want to keep lower-paying agencies in your client base, the most important factor is whether you're earning what you need or want to earn. If you are, I don't think it's inherently a bad idea to have clients paying different rates. Not all of my clients pay the same rate, and I'm OK with that. However, I think it's equally important to have a "red zone" rate that you never go below, (in his booklet I Am Worth It!), translator Jonathan Hine talks about this as your break-even point). Another factor to consider is your hourly rate; if you're very adept at translating surfing documents, you might be able to charge a lower per-word rate while still earning the same effective hourly rate as you do for higher-paying clients in other specializations. I also think it's a good idea to diversify your client base, as long as you're not all over the map. Having a mix of mainstream agencies, boutique agencies, and direct clients will help ensure that you always have a steady flow of interesting work.

Question: *When writing a cover letter to cold-contact an agency, who should you address it to? In some cases it's very easy to find names and email addresses of various members of management, so should you address it to the CEO, COO, Managing Director of Translation Services, or Human Resources Manager? Who would be most relevant?–Anonymous*

Answer: If you're applying to the agency by e-mail rather than using an online form, and you can't find the name of a specific person to whom to address the e-mail, just address it to the agency. Like "To the attention of Klingon Translations, Inc." That way, your e-mail doesn't look like spam and it's clearly personalized, but you're not risking addressing it to someone who no longer works there or isn't involved with translator recruitment.

Question: *What should I do if I have already contacted one million agencies with my CV? Why don't they respond? How can I convince them to hire me? —Patrick Weill*

Answer: First of all, how many is one million? In all seriousness, remember that applying to agencies is essentially cold selling. Like any cold selling, you should expect a 1%-3% response rate, so even if you contacted 200 agencies, I would expect responses from no more than 2-6 of them, unless you were referred by a colleague, the agency is in your local area, etc. Also, it's important to personalize each application to whatever extent you can. If the agency allows you to attach a cover e-mail, address it to the agency by name (as mentioned above), and include some little detail about them ("I found your website while researching medical translation companies in the

Chicago area," etc.). If you apply via an online form, use any field you can find (Additional Information, Comments, etc.) to add a personalized message. And don't count on getting a response on the first try; if you get *any* response other than an auto-responder, even "Thanks for your application, we'll keep it on file in case we need you," write the sender a handwritten thank-you note. Follow up at least every two weeks to a month until the agency either responds or asks you to stop contacting them, which they'll do if they really don't want to work with you.

Question: *I'm a French native speaker. I translate from Spanish and English to French. In my résumé you can read that I have a Bachelor's Degree in Spanish, and I worked in Spain for many years, in a multinational company. French, Spanish and English have been my working languages for more than 15 years. I'm also a member of the ProZ.com Certified PRO network, in the language pair Spanish to French. I guess that when you look at my resume, it looks that I'm more reliable in Spanish than in English! Indeed, I get many more translations from Spanish than from English into French. I know that my English is not perfect, but I've worked on my résumé and cover letter with a native English teacher. So, my question is: How can agencies trust me? What should I do to get them to believe in my competence in translating from English into French? —Alexandra Le Deun*

Answer: First off, I'm wondering whether you've actually experienced this as a problem with your agency clients (them not trusting you to translate from English), or whether you just fear that it could be a problem? In general, I think that 15 years of experience should be enough to satisfy an agency's concerns about your source languages, especially if you pass their tests. I do think that some agencies are (justifiably) wary of translators who work into their non-native language, but for source languages, it would surprise me if an agency wouldn't be swayed by a 15-year track record. If you are experiencing this as an actual problem, I would try to get some external assessment of your English skills; take the TOEFL or the IELTS, or one of the tests offered by Language Testing International or a similar entity. That should give you an assessment of your English skills that you can then include on your resume. I often suggest that option to people who acquired their language skills in non-traditional ways (i.e. by living or working in foreign countries rather than going to school).

Question: *How can I, as a beginning freelance translator, show the agencies my skills and make them inclined to work with me? What is the best way to catch their attention and stand out from all the offers they receive?* —*Amira Ben Mhenni*

Answer: That's a big question, and it really depends on the agencies you're applying to. Very large agencies are very transactional to work with: they will base their assessment mostly on your results on their tests, and you'll go into the pool of translators for your language pair who are contacted when they have a new project. With big agencies, it's mostly a matter of passing their tests, then waiting for them to contact you, but it can't hurt to follow up: send a handwritten note if you have the name of a specific person, otherwise check in every few weeks by e-mail until they send you something. With higher-quality agencies, it's more nuanced. The agencies you *really* want to work with are a) less likely to take a chance on a beginner, and b) more likely to be fully-staffed and not really looking for new translators; you have to wait until one of their regular translators leaves, or the agency gets a new client, in order to get work from them. In that case, do everything you can to stay at the top of their minds: handwritten note, send an e-mail checking in at least once a month, put a Google Alert on the agency's name in case there's something about them in the business news that you want to follow up on. As a beginner, it's also a good idea to work the local market—try to get informational interviews with any agencies in your local area, and try to attend in-person events organized by translators' associations so that you can meet potential clients there. Another good source of work for beginners is referrals and overflow work from more experienced translators. So, make sure to also network with other translators in your language pair and establish yourself as competent, energetic, and reliable so that they'll think of you when a client needs a referral.

Question: *Are there certain types of clients you can generally only access via agencies? For example, if I want to translate for US government agencies (on a freelance basis), are translation agencies the only way to go? I imagine there are various other types of clients that generally only purchase translation services from agencies for one reason or another.* —*Anonymous*

Answer: I hesitate to apply the terms "always" or "never" to any kind of translation work, but I do think there are certain types of clients that are *much more likely* to use agencies than freelancers. Fortunately, the procurement process for most government agencies is fairly transparent, because they're taxpayer-funded. For example, you can apply to be a freelance translator for the US Department of State, here. Government agencies are generally required to specify how they procure pretty much everything, so you should be able to find that information out, either online or by calling them. In general, I think that specializations where the end clients are often huge companies (software and pharmaceuticals come to mind) are more likely to be dominated by agencies. It's going to be tough—perhaps not impossible, but tough—to break into a Microsoft or a Novartis as a freelancer, unless your target clients have in-house translation departments that are used to working with freelancers. In those kinds of sectors, I think you need to either sleuth out which agencies those big companies work with, or aim for smaller, more boutique-type companies that are more likely to work with freelancers.

Question: *My question is how to find a central contact in a large agency when you deal with many different project managers? I've found it difficult to get a good flow of work—it's either all on or all off—so having a central contact could be useful. —Angela Eldering*

Answer: Well, the first question would be whether the agency *has* a centralized way of managing work that is sent out to freelancers. That would seem to work to both their and your advantage, but many clients—agencies and direct clients—seem to work in relatively siloed ways that don't involve a central system for assigning projects. That being said, I would just ask: tell your project managers, "I really enjoy working with your company, and I'm thrilled to be receiving so much work from you. I wonder if there is a way—for example a central contact for freelancers—to let you know my availability on a weekly or daily basis, so that you know what volume I'm available to take on?" That puts a positive spin on it (you're trying to help them out), and I think they'll get the point!

Question: *When just starting out as a freelance translator and you have no or close to no experience. How do you actually make an agency try your work, even for a test translation? How do you market yourself and your skills when you are new, without prior record or references – except studies? Marketing your work for free may not be a good idea, if you would get a job or several jobs it might be hard to start charging at some point? —Ann-Charlotte Storer*

Answer: When you're starting out, you want to first make sure that your translation skills are at a professional level: take the practice test for a translator certification exam, or pay a professional translator to evaluate your skills. Assuming the results from those assessments are positive, you have a few options as a complete newbie: apply to large agencies that base their hiring largely on their own tests, apply to local agencies that you can meet with in person to establish yourself as reliable and trustworthy, and network with more experienced translators who might be in a position to refer work to you. Also take advantage of anywhere you can meet potential clients in person, such as local or national translators' association events. It's equally important to just keep plugging away at it: if you are planning to work 40 hours a week as a translator, then force yourself to work those 40 hours even when you have little to no work at the beginning. Market, market, market. Join LinkedIn groups and actively participate in them. Work on your website. Read translation blogs. Take professional development courses in your specializations. Take writing and editing classes. Volunteer for your local translators' association. All of those things will be additional factors in convincing agencies to take a chance on a newbie!

Question: *I work almost exclusively with agencies out of choice. When I took maternity leave, obviously the PMs had to turn to other translators and I had a slow year when I went back to work, until they gave me the same level of work as before. I was wondering whether you had any tips for standing out and ensuring that the PM will always think of you first (apart from top-notch work of course!) You've talked about gifts and handwritten notes to direct clients but is there anything you would recommend for agency PMs? For example, would you recommend going to see them in person to say hi if in their area? I work with an agency in Prague and went on holiday there but wasn't sure if I would just be getting in the way by visiting them. —Julia Maitland*

Answer: When it comes to the question of, "Why isn't X agency sending me more work?" I think that we translators tend to overthink it (I must have made a horrible mistake on a translation, I must have said something that offended the PM, etc.) when in reality the situation is much simpler. PMs tend to gravitate to translators who nearly always accept the projects that the PM offers, deliver high-quality work, and meet their deadlines. Most PMs have their go-to translators: the people they *always* contact first. If someone tends not to be available, or not as available as the PM needs, they're not going to be the go-to person. So, when you went on maternity leave, you fell off that list and it took a while to work your way back up, which I think is to be expected. However I do think there are things you can do to further solidify your relationships with your agency clients: visiting them in person is definitely a good idea. When I do that, I try to put some parameters on it ("I'll be in your area and wondered if I could stop by quickly to say hello and meet some of your staff?") so that it doesn't sound like a huge time commitment on their part. I also think that when you prefer to work with agencies, you're always riding the line between wanting to be that go-to person, and knowing that you don't want one client—of any flavor—making up 80% of your work volume, and that's a balancing act that only you can handle.

Question: *Do you think it's necessary to have your own website if you're only really interested in marketing to agencies? —Grace Horsley*

Answer: It depends on what type of agency you're talking about. For large and very large agencies, I don't think a website is necessary; they're not going to cultivate a personal relationship with you, and will base their hiring largely or perhaps exclusively on their own tests. For smaller, boutique-type agencies, I think a website is a big plus. Even if your website's SEO is not powerful enough to attract clients to you, it's a good resource to send to potential clients, and to have in your e-mail signature for when you send out inquiries by e-mail.

Question: *How can I protect myself against payment delays, and what should I do if an agency doesn't pay me after the job is done? – Antonio Jorge Santos*

Answer: First, you need to vet your agency clients' credit-worthiness before you work for them. The best resources for that are Payment Practices or the ProZ Blue Board; of the two, I find Payment Practices to be more comprehensive and a membership is only $20 per year. But if you already have the ProZ paying membership, the Blue Board should be included in that. Before you ever work for an agency, check their rating there to at least ensure that you're not working for an agency that is known to be non-paying. If an agency ever doesn't pay you or pays significantly late (which Payment Practices defines as more than 10 days late), you should report that on one of those sites. And many agencies are now moving over to online invoicing systems where you can track exactly where your invoice is in the payment cycle. I think that the bigger problem for most translators is not non-paying clients, but slow-paying clients—that client where there always seems to be some snafu (finance person is on vacation, checks are only cut on certain days of the week, invoice slipped through the cracks, etc.). It's up to you how to handle that. As long as those clients do eventually pay, one option is simply to keep enough of a cash buffer in your business account that one late payment isn't a huge deal. Another option is to require clients to pay electronically rather than by paper check—something that I think more freelancers are moving toward—which at least eliminates the variable of the check having to be prepared and mailed. Another option is to send those clients some periodic reminders along the way, i.e. "Just wanted to remind you that invoice XXX for $Y is coming due on X date, let me know if you anticipate any delays in the payment." Personally, as long as a client always pays without a major delay, I am fairly tolerant of payments being a week or two late. But it's also true that an agency wouldn't see a one-week delay as "no big deal" when you're sending them a translation, so it's OK to press them to stick to the terms you agreed on.

Question: *I get the impression that a translator looking for agency work MUST go through the Work for Us/Careers page of the agency's website and never ever write them directly. If you've combed through the website with a fine-tooth comb and know that they have no such section, is it ever OK to write them at the email address on their website? (Especially if you see via ProZ and Payment Practices that they're active and working with translators from all over.) I've noticed that some agencies just don't have this open call on their websites, even over a period of years– maybe forever (while others don't temporarily, and then add it or add it back later, maybe depending on their need for freelancers). Should this be interpreted as their not wanting to hear from translators, or is it worth trying? And if you do write them, should you just send your CV and cover letter like normal without apologizing for your boldness, or should you first ask if it would be OK to send those materials? —Anonymous*

Answer: You're correct that agencies are in the business of hiring translators, otherwise they wouldn't be able to sell translations. But it's also true that some agencies are so flooded with applications that they may—temporarily or permanently—remove that information from their website. For example I work for at least one boutique agency that hires *only* through referrals from their existing translators. If you can't find any way to apply via the agency's website, I would send an e-mail to their general inquiry address (info@ or whatever you can find), and *only* ask, "Are you accepting applications from freelancers in my language pair and specializations?" Or call them and ask the same thing. I would not send your materials without inquiring as to whether the agency is hiring.

Question: *Yesterday I got a phone call from a PM of a potential new client. She asked me what my rate was for the services she required and I said X. She then asked me whether I could initially work for 50%–75% of X and in my head I flipped. I politely replied that no, there was no way I would agree to that. Without berating the client for their mindless cheekiness, how could I tackle such a situation in a more positive way in the future? —Anna Lycett*

Answer: I'm going to disagree with you here, in the sense that I don't see this as "mindless cheekiness" on the client's part, I just see it as the client's expression of the market segment that they've chosen, which is not the one that you've chosen. While I do (absolutely) agree that it *is* aggravating to be asked if you could lower your rate by half (of course not!), or to be treated as if you're the one with no clue about prevailing rates in the translation market (you wouldn't be charging your rates if no clients would pay them, right?), or to see other translators working for rock-bottom rates, it's also not worth getting emotional about. The client positions their work at a certain price point, and so do you. If they choose to compete on price or to make price a major selling point for their work, that's their decision. When I get those types of inquiries, I normally say something like, "Because I'm busy all the time at my regular rates, I'm unable to offer discounts at this time. But please keep me in mind if you ever have projects with larger budgets." Then I just leave it at that. It's also true that the shifts in our industry—largely driven by technology, globalization, and the increasing volume of freelancers—mean that there are a lot more people willing to work for a lot less money. So, never assume that a client won't find a translator who's willing to work for a lot less than you charge. Again, you can't control that—although it's certainly worth trying to help those translators see that they're devaluing not only their own work, but the work of everyone else in the industry. There are clients out there at all price points. So when a lowballing client comes knocking on your door, simply stand firm, pleasantly offer to work with them at your regular rates, and move on.

About the author

Corinne McKay, CT is an American Translators Association-certified French to English translator. She has worked as a full-time freelancer since 2002, for clients in the international development, corporate communications, and content marketing sectors. She also translates non-fiction books, and her translation of Erhard Loretan and Jean Ammann's *Night Naked: A Climber's Autobiography*, published by Mountaineers Books, was short-listed for the 2017 Boardman Tasker award for mountain literature. In addition to her own translation work, Corinne has taught classes and written books for other freelance translators since 2005. *How to Succeed as a Freelance Translator*, her business how-to guide for freelance translators, has sold over 10,000 copies and has become a go-to reference for the translation industry. Her blog, Thoughts on Translation, won the 2016 ProZ.com Community Choice Award for best blog about translation. Corinne can be reached at corinne@translatewrite.com.

For more translation-related information, advice, books, and courses, visit Corinne McKay's blog, Thoughts on Translation.